Who Has This Tail?

Laura Hulbert
illustrated by Erik Brooks

Henry Holt and Company · New York

Who has this tail?

A spider monkey has this tail.

A spider monkey uses its tail
to hang on to branches.

Who has this tail?

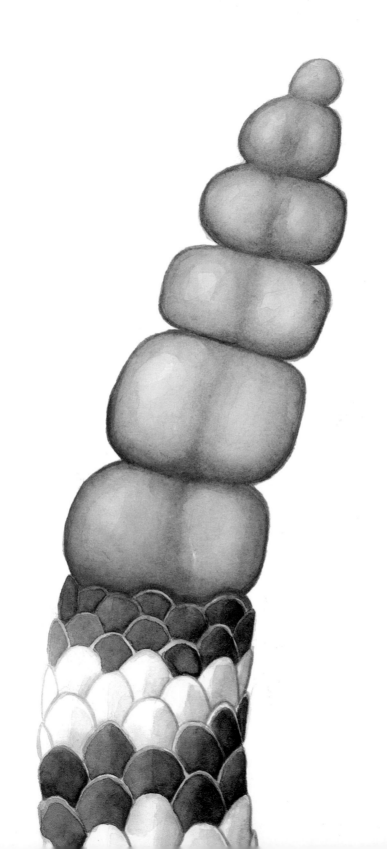

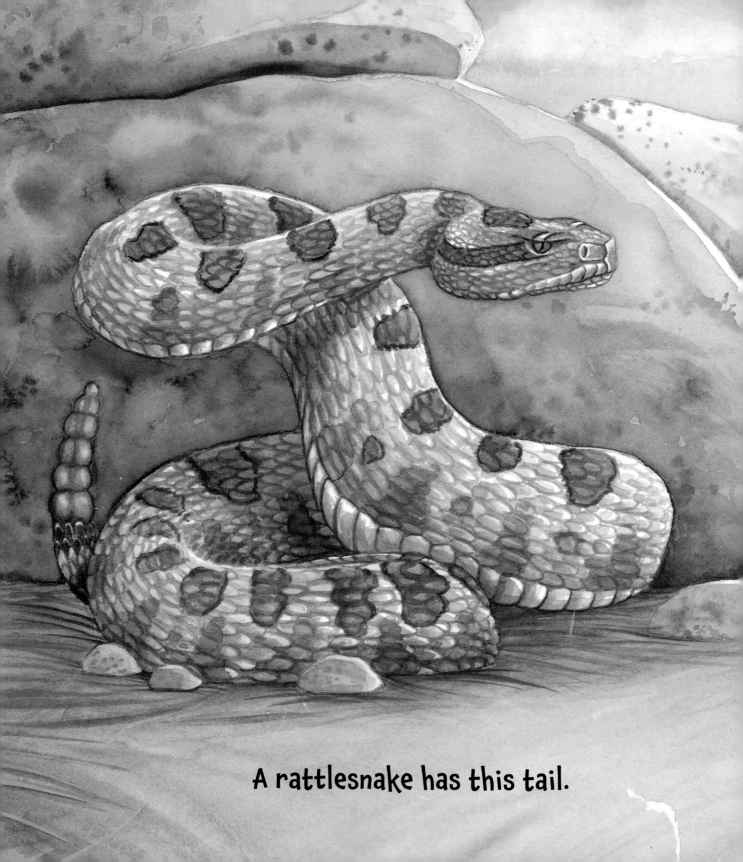

A rattlesnake has this tail.

A rattlesnake uses its tail to warn its enemies.

Who has this tail?

A shark has this tail.

A shark uses its tail to push
itself through the water.

Who has this tail?

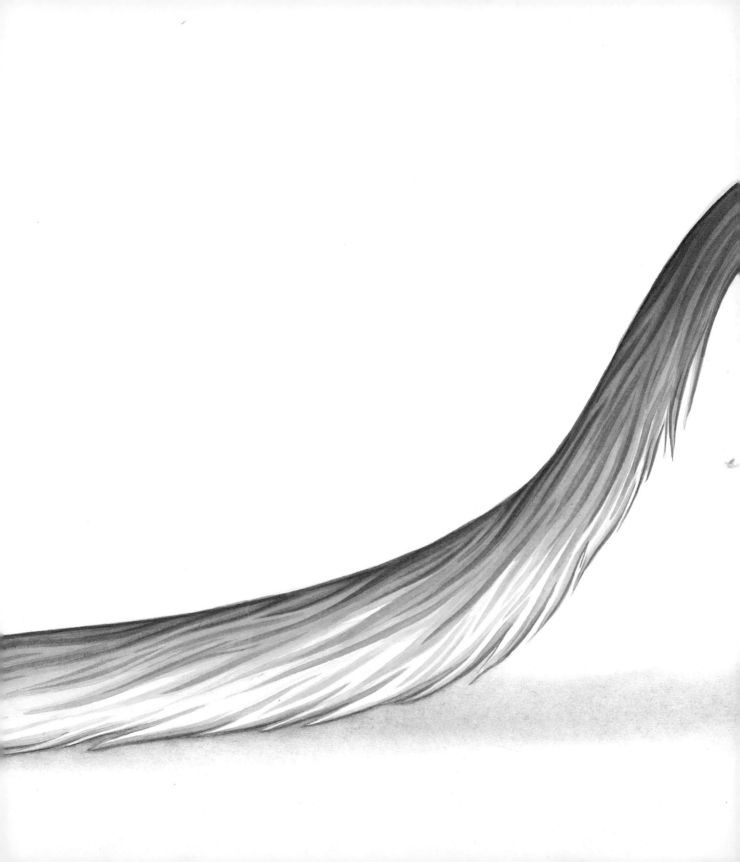

A gerbil has this tail.

A gerbil uses its tail to balance on its back legs.

Who
has this
tail?

A horse has this tail.

A horse uses its tail
to flick away flies.

Who has this tail?

A scorpion has this tail.

A scorpion uses its tail to sting its prey.

Who has this tail?

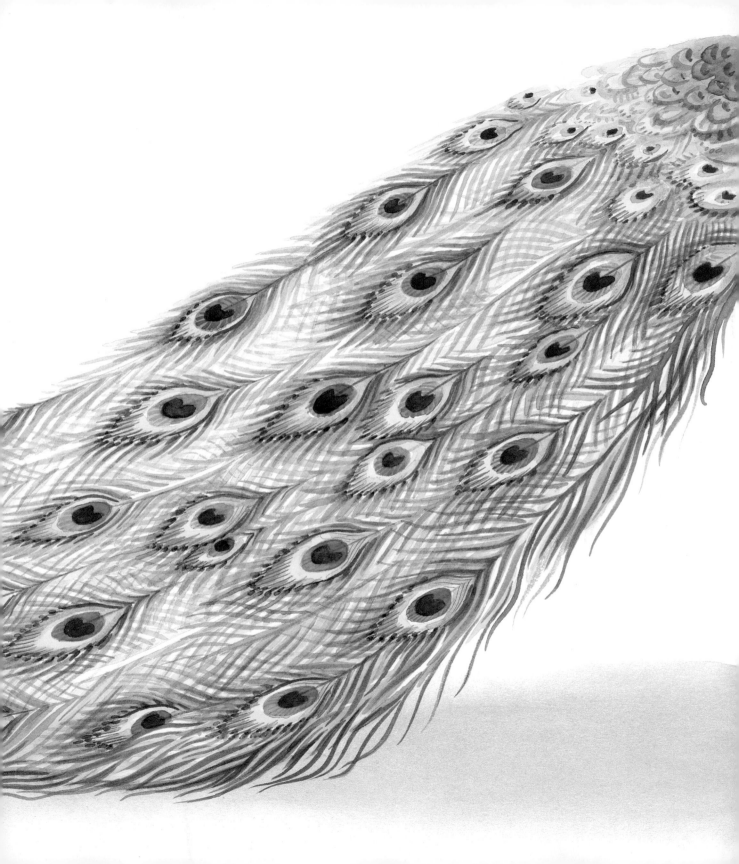

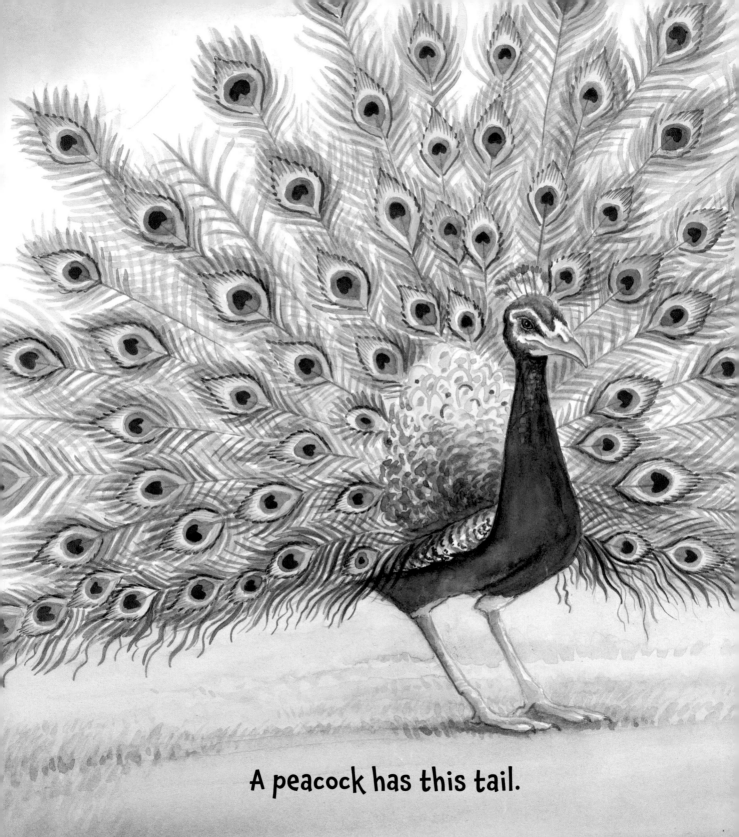

A peacock has this tail.

A peacock uses its tail
to attract a mate.

Who has this tail?

An Arctic fox has this tail.

An Arctic fox uses its tail
to stay warm when it sleeps.

Who has this tail?

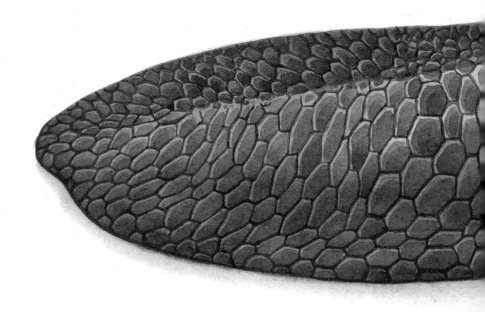

A beaver has this tail.

A beaver uses its tail to steer in the water.

We have

Who

has

open here

these

tails?

open here

these tails!

For Mary
—L. H.

For Will, who landed tailfirst
—E. B.

Henry Holt and Company, LLC
Publishers since 1866
175 Fifth Avenue
New York, New York 10010
mackids.com

Library of Congress Cataloging-in-Publication Data
Hulbert, Laura.
Who has this tail? / Laura Hulbert ; illustrated by Erik Brooks. — 1st ed.
p.   cm.
ISBN 978-0-8050-9429-9 (hc)
1. Tail—Juvenile literature. I. Brooks, Erik, ill. II. Title.
QL950.6.H85 2012   590—dc23   2011034056

First Edition—2012
The artist used watercolor on paper to create the illustrations for this book.
Printed in China by Macmillan Production Asia Ltd.,
Kwun Tong, Kowloon, Hong Kong (Vendor Code: 10)

1 3 5 7 9 10 8 6 4 2